Travel Through
China

Lynn Huggins-Cooper

QED Publishing

Copyright © QED Publishing 2007

First published in the UK in 2007 by
QED Publishing
A Quarto Group company
226 City Road
London EC1V 2TT

www.qed-publishing.co.uk

A Catalogue record for this book is available from the British Library.

ISBN 978 1 84538 660 3

Written by Lynn Huggins-Cooper
Designed by Rahul Dhiman (Q2A Media)
Editor Honor Head
Picture Researcher Pritika Ghura (Q2A Media)

Publisher Steve Evans
Creative Director Zeta Davies
Senior Editor Hannah Ray

Printed and bound in China

Picture credits

Key: t = top, b = bottom, m = middle,
l = left, r = right, FC = front cover

Dimitrios Kaisaris/ **Shutterstock**: 4t, **Index Stock Imagery**/ **Photolibrary**: 4, 12t, 19t, tamir niv/
Shutterstock: 6, Photomediacom/ **Shutterstock**: 7t, wu xiao bai/ **Shutterstock**: 7b, **Nordic
Photos**/ **Photolibrary**: 8, Ray Laskowitz/ **Lonely Planet Images**: 9t, Chris Mellor/ **Lonely Planet
Images**: 9m, Bruce B/ **Lonely Planet Images**: 10, Imagestate Ltd/ **Photolibrary**: 11t, **Photonica
Inc**/ **Photolibrary**: 11b, 15b, Nicholas Pavloff/ **Lonely Planet Images**: 12b, Bill Wassman/ **Lonely
Planet Images**: 13t, Gautier Willaume/ **Istockphoto**: 13m, Greg Elms/ **Lonely Planet Images**:
14t, Paul Barton/**Corbis**: 14b, Phil Weymouth/ **Lonely Planet Images**: 15t, Diana Mayfield/ **Lonely
Planet Images**: 16b, Richard I'Anson/ **Lonely Planet Images**: 16–17t, Lee Foster/ **Lonely Planet
Images**: 17b, Chinatiger/ **Bigstockphoto**: 18, Gergely Bényi/ **Shutterstock**: 19b, Hsin Chu, Taiwan:
20t, **Photo Researchers, Inc.**/ **Photolibrary**: 20b, Craig Pershouse/ **Lonely Planet Images**: 22b,
Jon Arnold Images/ **Photolibrary**: 23t, **Panorama Media (Beijing) Ltd**/ **Photolibrary**: 23m, 27b,
Garry Weare/ **Lonely Planet Images**: 24b, Peter Arnold Images Inc/ **Photolibrary**: 25t, **Animals
Animals / Earth Scenes**/ **Photolibrary**: 25b, 27t, Keren Su/ **Lonely Planet Images**: 26b.

Words in **bold** can be found in the glossary on page 31.

Contents

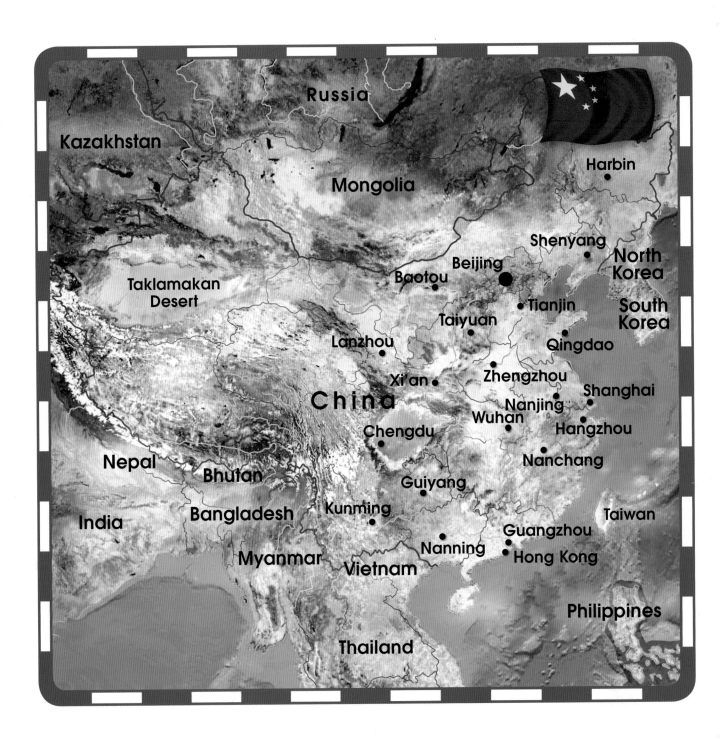

Russia

Kazakhstan

Mongolia

Harbin

Shenyang

North
Korea

Beijing

Baotou

Tianjin

South
Korea

Taiyuan

Taklamakan
Desert

Qingdao

Lanzhou

Zhengzhou

Xi'an

Shanghai

China

Nanjing

Wuhan

Hangzhou

Chengdu

Nanchang

Nepal

Guiyang

Bhutan

Kunming

Taiwan

India

Bangladesh

Guangzhou

Nanning

Hong Kong

Myanmar

Vietnam

Philippines

Thailand

Where in the world is China?

China is a huge country, divided up into areas called **provinces**. It covers most of East Asia, and it is the fourth-largest country in the world. As it is so large, it has many different **climates**, from **temperate** to **sub-arctic**. China is home to people of 56 different **ethnic groups**. Han is the largest group, making up around 85 per cent of the **population**.

One in five of all the people in the world live in China. The population is growing by an incredible 15 million people each year. The government introduced a 'one child' policy in 1979 so that people did not have large families, which would add to the overpopulation problem.

China includes Hong Kong, which was handed over from Britain to the People's Republic of China in 1997. Hong Kong is quite different from the rest of China. It is very western as a result of being part of Britain for over 150 years.

Did you know?

OFFICIAL NAME: People's Republic of China

SURROUNDING COUNTRIES: Russia, India, Afghanistan, Bhutan, Myanmar, Kazakhstan, North Korea, Kyrgyzstan, Laos, Macau, Mongolia, Nepal, Pakistan, Tajikistan and Vietnam

SURROUNDING SEAS AND OCEANS: Pacific Ocean, South China Sea

CAPITAL: Beijing

AREA: 9 596 960sq km

POPULATION: 1 303 701 000

LIFE EXPECTANCY: 71 years

RELIGIONS: Taoism, Buddhism, Islam

LANGUAGES: Chinese (Mandarin), Cantonese

CLIMATE: ranges from desert to **tropical** to sub-arctic

HIGHEST MOUNTAIN: Mount Everest in the Himalayas (8850m high).

MAJOR RIVERS: Yangtze River (6380km long),

What is China like?

There are many different landscapes throughout China. There are hills, **plains**, and **river deltas** in the east and deserts, high **plateaus** and mountains in the west.

Deadly desert

The Taklimakan desert in the west of China is the second-largest desert in the world. It is known as the 'desert of death' as it is so dry. The Gobi desert is also in China and Southern Mongolia. The grains of sand in the Gobi desert are smooth and round, unlike typical sand which is coarse and irregular. In very dry weather conditions, the sand slides down the dunes and the grains bump together making a booming noise, like spooky music!

Legend has it that the Gobi desert was created when a magical Mongolian chief was being chased by the Chinese army. He cast a spell and the land behind him died, leaving the desert.

In summer, the temperature in the Gobi desert rises to a blistering 57°C, and in winter temperatures can drop to -60°C.

Varied climate

The climate in China is very varied. In Hainan, in the south, they have warm tropical weather and you only need light clothes. In Manchuria, in the north, you need lots of warm clothes because the climate is sub-arctic. This means the temperatures are very low, as low as -30°C in the winter, and the summers are short and warm.

Hainan province is famous for its stunning scenery and beautiful beaches. Tianya Haijiao and Dadonghai are two well-known beaches and many people visit every year to sunbathe and to swim in the sea.

Where people live

Although China has many big, busy cities, 70 per cent of the people live in **rural** areas. This is because people prefer to settle and live where the climate is mild and food crops can be grown. Shandong province is on the east coast and its climate is very mild. About 91 million people live here because the weather is so pleasant.

The huge Mount Everest is on the China/Nepal border.

Getting around

In the past, rickshaws were used to carry rich and important people through the streets of China. Today they are used by tourists.

China has many airports and a good system of internal flights, which makes travelling across the huge country much quicker. Many people also travel by car. Large cities such as Shanghai and Beijing have big **freeways,** but there are many cars, and traffic jams are often a problem. The traffic also causes high levels of air pollution. It can make travelling unpleasant and some people wear anti-pollution masks when they travel.

There are many fast, busy roads in China but they are often clogged with traffic. There are around 15 000 000 cars in China.

Travelling by train

The larger Chinese cities have underground railways which are very busy. They have special guards to squash people into the carriages during the rush hour. But the underground is a great way to get around quickly and to avoid the traffic jams. China also has a large rail network above ground, with **sleeper cars** for long-distance travel.

On your bike!

Bicycles are very popular in China. There are 300 million bikes whizzing about the country. Pedicabs are bikes with a passenger seat attached and these are used like taxis. There are also a few tourist rickshaws and sedan chairs. Rickshaws are small carts pulled by one person. A sedan chair is a compartment in which a person sits. The chair is then lifted up and carried by two people, one at either end.

Many people in China travel by bike. There are up to 10 million bicycles in Beijing alone!

YOU'VE GOT MAIL

Today, I went on a boat trip on a **junk** and visited the floating homes and shops in Hong Kong – what a way to travel! We went to a place called Aberdeen, which is an area of the harbour crammed with junks and **sampans**. About 6000 people live and work there. I bought a **jade** charm, which is very pretty, and some noodles for lunch – yum!
Su Ling

Major cities

China has many beautiful cities which contain an interesting mix of ancient monuments and modern buildings.

Beautiful Beijing

Beijing is the capital of the People's Republic of China. After Shanghai, it is the city with the second-largest population in China. The Forbidden City (or Forbidden Palace) at the centre of Beijing is a beautiful place which you can go and visit. It used to be the Imperial Palace, where the **emperors** who used to rule China lived, and is now a huge museum. It is listed by **UNESCO** as the largest collection of ancient wooden buildings in the world and it is a **World Heritage site**.

The Forbidden City has 800 buildings and over 8000 rooms.

Skyscraping city

Shanghai is on the banks of the Yangtze River Delta in Eastern China. It is China's largest city and the eighth-largest city in the world. There are many modern skyscrapers in Shanghai. The Oriental Pearl Tower is 468m tall and visitors can climb to the top to look at the views. There is a revolving restaurant, a science museum and a disco room as you travel up the tower.

Shanghai is a beautiful waterfront city. It is one of the world's busiest ports and became the largest cargo port in the world in 2005.

Hi! I went to Shanghai with Mum for a visit last week. It was the first time we've been. We went to the People's Park one morning and saw hundreds of people doing Tai Chi – a series of movements and exercises. Afterwards we went to the Oriental Pearl Tower and had lunch in the revolving restaurant. The views were amazing! Then we did some shopping. We went to the Xiangyang market, which is a great place to buy clothes, and then to Dongtai Lu market to buy some ornaments as presents. Mum spent hours looking at the antiques.

Love
Shushi

Many people practise Tai Chi to keep their bodies and minds fit and healthy.

Farming in China

Farming is very important in China. About two-thirds of the working population of China work in **agriculture** or with **livestock**. As you travel across China, you will see vast areas of farmland. China is the world's largest producer of rice, wheat, **soya beans** and cane sugar. It **exports** many of these products around the world and you can buy them in supermarkets as well as specialist shops.

This woman has to carry heavy buckets to water her crops.

Best crops

Rice is a big crop in China. It is grown in fields that are flooded and drained to help the rice grow. Water from rivers and streams is piped into the fields. Cotton and oilseeds are also widely grown, especially as **cash crops** for export. China has many mouths to feed and it is **self-sufficient** in cereal, fish and meat.

There are about 12 million yaks in China. They are used for milk, meat and their skins.

Fishermen catch fish to eat and sell. Fish is a very popular food in China.

My mum is a rice farmer. She has learned lots about how to grow better rice, in easier ways, from the Agricultural Broadcasting School. The school uses TV, audio and video recordings and computer programs to teach people who are scattered all over our huge country. Going to a college is hard for many people, as they live far away and cannot leave their fields to travel to study. The Agricultural Broadcasting School helps everyone to learn at home. Now my mum is growing new types of rice that are specially suited to our conditions. This will make it easier to grow good crops and means our village will have lots of rice to sell. My mum runs training classes for other farmers when they are not busy growing rice – so now everybody is learning.

Yin

The fields in which rice is grown are called paddy fields.

Food and drink

In China, lots of food is cooked in a wok, a special pan which is rounded rather than flat. It is used for stir-frying food such as noodles, bean sprouts and bamboo shoots. Stir-frying makes the food cook quickly and seals in vitamins. Food is also often steamed in special bamboo baskets.

Wontons are small dough parcels containing meat or vegetables. They are often served with soup.

This family is enjoying a meal of noodles. They are eating with chopsticks.

Tea is very popular in China. It can be bought in teashops and from special sellers in the street.

Woks can also be used for making stews and soups, as well as for stir-frying.

Something special

Different parts of China have different speciality dishes. Beijing is famous for roast duck, while Sichuan province is famous for food cooked with spices such as ginger, chilli and star anise, which grows in China. The city of Xi'an is famous for its dumplings, called jiaozi. There are many types and each type has a different shape depending on what is inside. Fillings include chicken and pork. Cantonese food, from the area around Guangzhou, is mildly spiced. It often includes fish and has a delicate flavour. Eastern-style food often includes fish, with dishes such as fish tail stew, hot-and-sour fish soup, steamed crabs and deep-fried fish with bamboo shoots.

Bowl and chopsticks

Food is often eaten from small bowls using chopsticks, which even small children are able to use. Travellers sometimes find it quite difficult to use chopsticks properly as it takes some practise!

It was my birthday yesterday and Mum took me and some of my friends out for a special meal. I had a vegetarian banquet and it was so delicious I wish my tummy held more! I had sweetcorn soup with seaweed, then deep-fried **tofu** with black bean sauce and fried rice. I had **lychees** for dessert. Lychees are my favourite but they look like eyeballs! I had Jasmine tea at the end of the meal which smelled wonderful —and tasted pretty good, too. Have you ever tried Jasmine tea?

Love

Huo

Famous sites

China has many beautiful, historic sites to visit. Some of them are many centuries old.

The pagoda forest

A pagoda is a temple which is shaped like a tall tower. There is a 'pagoda forest' at the Shaolin Temple in Henan province, where 220 brick and stone pagodas have been built as tombs for the monks and abbots of the temple. As you travel through the 'forest', you can see many **kung fu** masters and students demonstrating their skills to visitors.

Wonder wall

The Great Wall of China was built from the 5th century BCE to protect China from invasion from the fierce **nomadic** tribes of neighbouring Mongolia. It is 6400km long, and runs from the Shanhai Pass in the east to Lop Nur in the west.

The wall is built in very steep steps, and tourists get very tired trying to climb them!

Temple visits

In Qufu, in Shandong province, many tourists visit the Temple of Confucius, named after a famous teacher and thinker. The temple is made up of many buildings, and includes nine courtyards. There are 466 rooms and 54 gateways.

Today I visited the Great Wall. I saw one of the special forts built into the Wall and went inside. There are holes built into the wall which are about 30cm high. They were used to shoot arrows from when the wall was attacked. The wall was so long - it stretched away into the distance as far as I could see. A notice said that the wall is the largest structure ever built by people.

Chang

The clay figures are very lifelike. They are different heights and have hairstyles according to the rank of soldier they represent.

Clay army

In March 1974, farmers drilling a well to the east of Mount Lishan in Shaanxi province unearthed the **necropolis** of the Emperor Qin Shi Huang and found the first of what would eventually be nearly 9000 life-size **terracotta** warriors. This incredible army of red clay soldiers was created to guard the emperor in death. Each warrior was given a real weapon, such as a crossbow, spear or sword. Today, you can visit these warriors in the Museum of Qin Terracotta Warriors at Xi'an.

Art in China

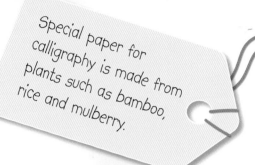

China has many different types of traditional art, including silk painting, calligraphy and embroidery. Chinese art is often highly detailed and very beautiful.

Beautiful writing

Chinese calligraphy is a very beautiful way of writing that has been done for thousands of years. It uses special solid blocks of ink, made from soot or oil smoke mixed with water. The writing is done with brushes, like a painting.

Sing a story

Chinese opera tells the stories of heroes and supernatural creatures. The actors have their faces painted with bright colours to make their features look bigger. Visitors can buy masks of the painted faces which can be used as ornaments.

Paper decorations

Paper was invented in China in the 1st century CE. Paper cuts are a traditional Chinese decoration. Using scissors or a special knife, an artist cuts a complicated picture of plants, animals or people into paper.

Paper cuts are used to decorate houses during festivals and holidays.

Embroidery and silk

Chinese embroidery usually shows pictures of beautiful women, dragons and cherry blossom. It has been created in China for centuries and tourists often buy embroidered objects to take home as souvenirs. Silk painting is also traditional in China and is used on screens, fans, kites and clothing.

I went to a kite festival yesterday! The sky was full of colourful kites in different shapes and designs. There were butterflies, birds, dragonflies, goldfish and even huge dragons. A Nantong whistle kite swooped right past my head! It shrieked really loudly. All the amazing kites I saw are made from thin bamboo sticks and silk or paper. Kite builders have to master 'the four skills'. That's making the frame, pasting on the silk, painting the silk – and then flying the kite!

Mei

A kite's bamboo frame has to be completely symmetrical so that the kite is evenly balanced. Then, the silk is hand painted.

Chinese exports

China **manufactures** many different types of goods that it exports all over the world. If you like playing computer or console games, it is likely that you have played some games that were made in China. Many games and toys come from Hong Kong. It is amazing to think how far your toys may have travelled before you play with them! China is famous for exporting many other things, too.

Silk road

Hundreds of years ago, long lines of carts travelled through Asia to other countries selling silk. The route they took was called the Silk Road. Today, many types of silk are still exported from China. If you visit China, you will see lots of brightly coloured silk clothing for sale.

Pearl place

China produces more pearls than any other country. Most of China's freshwater pearl farms are near the Yangtze River and are within 500km of Shanghai. Most of the pearls are made into jewellery but some are crushed and made into medicine or cosmetics.

Silk has been used to create these traditional-style Chinese costumes.

This pearl farmer is taking out the pearl which has been grown by this huge mussel.

Printing books

China has huge factories which print books in many different languages. Book companies from around the world send their books to China to be printed, where it is much cheaper.

Books are printed onto very long pieces of paper and then sliced up into sections to make pages.

Festivals and holidays

In China, there are many festivals and holidays, which are also celebrated by Chinese people who live in other countries around the world.

Happy New Year!

In late January or early February, Chinese New Year parties fill the streets with parades and dances. Businesses close so everyone can join in the fun. People in lion costumes dance through the streets, bringing blessings to businesses and homes that leave out offerings for the lion. Children wake up early to find small red envelopes containing sweets or money under their pillows.

Fireworks were invented in China. They are a very popular part of many celebrations.

Before a dragon boat enters a competition, it is 'brought to life' by painting eyes on the dragon's face in a special ceremony.

Lion dancers are accompanied by music played with gongs and drums. Firecrackers are set off to bring good luck.

Tuen Ng

In June, Tuen Ng, or the Dragon Boat festival, takes place all over East Asia. Wonderful boats, carved and painted to look like dragons, are raced across the water. Drums beat out a fast rhythm as the crews row the boats as quickly as they can to the finishing line. A famous Dragon Boat race takes place every year in Hong Kong, with teams from around the world taking part. Special rice dumplings called zongzi, made of sticky rice wrapped in bamboo or reed leaves, are cooked and eaten during Tuen Ng.

YOU'VE GOT MAIL

My family is having a party for New Year. We are going to see the lion dances and parades and then we are coming home to watch some fireworks and have a special meal. We are having lettuce wraps, spring rolls and sticky cake, which is like steamed fruit cake. It will be great fun!

love Cheng

The Himalayas

The Himalayan Mountains stretch 2600km across south-west China, northern Pakistan, Nepal, Bhutan and northern India. The Himalayas have been described as 'where the Earth meets the sky'. They are the world's highest mountain chain.

Top ten

The Himalayas contain an amazing nine of the ten highest peaks in the world. This includes Mount Everest, which is the highest mountain in the world at 8850m high, and K2, which is 8611m. Both of these mountains are on the border between China and Pakistan. Any areas of the Himalayas that are above 4880m have a very cold climate and are always covered in snow and ice. In the mountains, the air is very thin which makes it hard to breathe and people get tired very quickly. Climbing expeditions take oxygen with them to avoid this.

The highest parts of the Himalayas are covered in deep snow all year round.

Mountain habitats

When people think of the Himalayas, they think of cold mountains, but there are many different habitats in the Himalayan range including tropical forests and **sub-tropical** forests in the foothills. This means that there are wide varieties of animals and plants. Many of these animals, such as the red panda and the snow leopard, are very rare.

The red panda is also known as the wah because of the strange noise it makes.

Edmund Hillary and Tenzing Norgay were the first people to reach the top of Mount Everest, in 1953.

I am having a great time at Lugu Lake in the Himalayas, on the border between Sichuan province and Yannan province. The area is sometimes called The Kingdom of Women. The Mosuo people who live there believe women should be in charge of society and they all hold positions of power. Mum thinks this is very sensible!
Manika

Scientists believe there may only be 35 Amur leopards left in the wild, living in China's border regions and the far east of Russia.

The environment

China is a huge country with many different landscapes and habitats, but it faces a number of environmental challenges – from poor air quality to endangered animals. However, steps are being taken to solve some of these problems.

Dust storms

The Taklimakan desert has dust storms that can carry dust all over the world. In early December 2005, there was a terrible dust storm which blew sand across China, creating many health problems, such as asthma.

Beating the storms

There is a major dust storm in China almost every year. On the outskirts of Beijing, huge forests are being planted to improve the air quality and to prevent dust from creating more health problems. The forests help to put more oxygen into the air. Trees and bushes can also help to stop the dust from travelling too far as they act as a barrier and stop the dust from blowing across the country.

These golden monkeys live safely in a wildlife reserve near Beijing.

China takes the protection of pandas very seriously. Until 1997, the penalty for killing a panda was execution. Today, it is 20 years imprisonment.

Save the animals

We have been fundraising this term to help save endangered animals. I have chosen to study Przewalski's Horse, or the Takhi, which is the last wild horse left in the world. The Takhi disappeared from the Gobi desert in the 1960s, but a few were still held in zoos. A breeding programme has built up numbers, and the Takhi was reintroduced to the wild. There is now a herd of over 60 horses.

Lee

Nature reserves

Many endangered animals are found in China – over 385 threatened species according to the **IUCN Red List**. Some animals have been hunted nearly to **extinction**. Others are suffering as their habitats are destroyed by industry and building projects. China has created many nature reserves covering 117 million hectares (over 12 per cent of China) to give animals and plants a safe place to live. People are usually not allowed to build, cut down trees or hunt on nature reserves. Protecting habitats is helping to save endangered species such as the giant panda, golden monkey, Chinese alligator, Asiatic elephant, snow leopard and the Siberian tiger.

The Siberian Tiger is the largest member of the cat family. There are only 350–450 left in the wild and some of these can be found in north-east China.

Activity ideas

1 Using travel brochures, cut out pictures and make a poster to show the image China gives to tourists. What ideas and images do travel agents use to 'sell' China as a holiday destination?

2 Visit a supermarket and look for food and products that have come from China. Have all the foods identified as 'Chinese food', such as noodles, prawn crackers, etc. actually been processed in China?

3 Plan a holiday to China. Choose ten places, monuments, etc. that you would like to visit. Why did you choose those places?

4 Using books and the Internet, find out about some of the wildlife found in China, and make a fact file. Create sections about different animals – anything you find interesting!

5 Imagine that you are travelling across China. Write an imaginary diary about your journey. What do you see? Who do you meet? Does anything funny happen to you? You could add drawings, too.

6 Write a tourist leaflet describing a city in China. You are trying to encourage people to visit the country, so use exciting and appealing language.

7 Make a model of The Great Wall of China from papier mâché. Find out more about the wall first from http://www.enchantedlearning.com/subjects/greatwall/

8 Do a Web search about the floating city in Aberdeen, Hong Kong. Make a list of the facts you find, and write a presentation to tell others about it. You could print out pictures to accompany your talk.

9 Find out more about Chinese New Year. Write a report as though you spent Chinese New Year in Shanghai, and experienced it for yourself.

10 Make a dragon puppet for Chinese New Year. Concertina fold a brightly coloured strip of paper – this will be your dragon's body. Make a head from a small box and tape it to the front of the body. Cut a tail out of thin card, and tape it to the end of the body. Tape a lolly stick to the front of your dragon, just behind and underneath its head. Tape another lolly stick beneath its tail. Decorate the dragon with paint, tissue, crêpe paper and sequins. Hold the lolly sticks and make your dragon dance!

11 Find other places on the same **latitude** as China. Find out if the average temperatures are the same, or if they differ. Plot the results on a chart to compare the temperatures in the different countries.

12 Make a 3D map of China using papier mâché. Draw the rough shape on a sheet of card, and add pieces of crumpled paper, glued firmly in place, to build up the land. Don't forget the Himalayas! Coat the model in PVA glue, and cover the whole model carefully with a strips of tissue paper. Repeat this step until you have a smooth surface and leave to dry. Then paint and label your model with major cities, rivers and mountains.

13 Find a recipe for regional food from China – the Internet is a good source. With an adult, cook the food and eat a Chinese meal. You could also buy some examples of ready-made Chinese foods and sample them, before reviewing them and displaying the reports of the 'food critics'!

NOTE FOR ADULTS:
Please ensure that children do not suffer from any food allergies before making or eating any food.

14 Make a fact file about the Terracotta Warriors – and then make a small model of a warrior from clay.

15 Carry out research using the Internet, magazines and newspapers to find out more about the problem of dust being carried across China from the Taklimakan desert. Use your information to think of ideas to solve the problem. Can you dream up an invention that would help?

16 With an adult, visit a Chinese supermarket and see the variety of food on offer. Compare the food there with the food you eat. What is different?

17 Find out more information on how pearls are made. Write a report about how Chinese pearls get from mussel to necklace.

18 Make a mini Chinese kite using cocktail sticks and tissue paper. Borrow a book from the library or search on the Internet to find out how. Discover more about Chinese kites at www.wfkitemuseum.com.

19 Have a go at making your own paper cuts. You need a simple shape to start with. Use brightly coloured paper to make your paper cut, and tape it to a window when you are finished to show it off. Find out more about paper cuts on: http://www.isaacnet.com/culture/papercut.htm

20 Make a dragon boat that floats! Using scrap bits and pieces, make a dragon boat that will float in a tub of water. It's harder than it looks, because adding a dragon head and neck makes the boat 'front heavy. How can you balance the weight so the boat floats in the water? Don't forget to decorate your boat!

Glossary

agriculture The production of crops or livestock.

cash crop Something which is grown to sell.

climate The usual weather conditions of a particular place or region.

emperors Name given to the rulers of China, from 221 BCE to 1912.

ethnic groups A group of people who identify with each other, usually because of a shared ancestry. People within an ethnic group often speak the same language and have similar customs.

exports When someone ships goods to other countries.

extinction When a type of animal or plant dies out completely.

freeways Large, wide roads.

IUCN Red List A list of endangered species produced by the International Union for the Conservation of Nature and Natural Resources.

jade A green, semi-precious gemstone.

junk A traditional Chinese boat with square sails.

kung fu A Chinese martial art

latitude Distance from the equator (an imaginary circle around the middle of the earth, shown on most maps).

livestock Farmed animals such as sheep, goats and cows.

lychees A fruit with sweet, white flesh and a rough, pink skin.

manufactures Makes or creates.

necropolis A prehistoric or historic burial ground or cemetery.

nomadic Travelling from place to place.

plains Flat, open areas of land.

plateaus High flat areas of land.

population People who live in a particular place.

provinces Districts or regions within a country.

river deltas Flat plains at the mouth of a river.

rural In the countryside.

sampans Traditional Chinese boats with a flat bottom and oars.

self-sufficient Able to provide totally for itself.

sleeper cars Carriages on trains for sleeping in on long journeys.

soya beans A type of pulse used in cooking.

sub-arctic The region immediately south of the Arctic Circle.

sub-tropical Nearly tropical.

temperate Weather which is not too hot nor too cold.

terracotta Red clay.

tofu High-protein food made from curdled soybean milk.

tropical Very hot and humid.

UNESCO United Nations Educational, Scientific and Cultural Organization.

World Heritage site Important historic site as recognized by UNESCO.

Index